LITTLE BOOK OF

BOTTEGA VENETA

To Mami

Published in 2024 by Welbeck
An imprint of the Welbeck Publishing Group
Offices in: London – 20 Mortimer Street, London W1T 3JW &
Sydney – Level 17, 207 Kent St, Sydney NSW 2000 Australia
www.welbeckpublishing.com

Design and layout © Welbeck Non-Fiction Limited 2024
Text © Frances Solá-Santiago 2024

A CIP catalogue for this book is available from the British Library.

ISBN 978-1-80279-642-1

Printed in China

10 9 8 7 6 5 4 3 2 1

LITTLE BOOK OF

BOTTEGA VENETA

The story of the iconic design house

FRANCES SOLÁ-SANTIAGO

WELBECK

CONTENTS

INTRODUCTION

INTRODUCTION

"Bottega Veneta is a bag company. It means that you go places – it's as simple as that" – Matthieu Blazy, Bottega Veneta creative director

Few names have more resonance in fashion than Bottega Veneta, with its stealth wealth approach and strong focus on craftsmanship. Yet, compared to many of its luxury and leather goods counterparts, which have centuries-old histories, Bottega Veneta is a young house with a little over 50 years in existence. Still, since its founding in 1966, the brand has grown from a small shop in Venice to a global luxury empire that spans from ready-to-wear and footwear to jewellery and leather goods. And its history reads like a revolving door of creators, artisans and business people who have all attempted to figure out: *What is Bottega Veneta?*

What we know of Bottega Veneta today is the result of constant evolution, which started with its co-founders in Venezia and has seen multiple creative directors, design teams,

OPPOSITE In 2021, Bottega Veneta's signature green shade took over as the de facto logo of the brand.

BELOW A lineup of
models walking in
Bottega Veneta's
Autumn 2022
runway show.

collaborators and ownership. But at its core, Bottega Veneta is a leather goods brand that is continuously reimagining what accessories can be for a customer who basks in carrying a piece of heritage – no logos included. And yet, throughout its attempts at ready-to-wear – some successful, others perhaps better considered as great first drafts – have also shown that a leather goods house doesn't have to stick with one category. Instead, it can bring its leather weaving techniques and aesthetic sensibility to everyday clothing that can captivate the fashion zeitgeist. Over the last few years, Bottega Veneta has achieved massive mainstream success, thanks to newcomer

creative directors rethinking what the luxury house can be in an increasingly digitized and globalized fashion industry, and making it one of the most sought-after brands today.

Ultimately, Bottega Veneta is an example that simply doesn't have to mean basic, and that indeed, to quote the house's years-old motto, your own initials can be enough. It's also a mix of tradition and futurism; material maximalism and aesthetic minimalism; sober and bold. Its intricate techniques and house codes, which have continued to evolve as new creative directors take over, reject the idea that, in order to sell, a brand has to shed its heritage.

BELOW Bottega Veneta leather briefcases, as shown to the press in 1979.

OPPOSITE Actor
Margot Robbie
wears a green dress
by Mattieu Blazy's
Bottega Veneta
in 2022.

BELOW A Bottega
Veneta storefront.

OVERLEAF Jodie
handbags inside on
display at a Bottega
Veneta store.

This book is a recollection of the milestones and transformations that led to Bottega Veneta's rise as a global fashion force – known for its viral accessories, luxurious leather handbags and minimalist clothing rooted in Italian heritage – from its crafty beginnings to its billion-euro successes. It's also a look at the people who have grown Bottega Veneta into the brand we know today, and who have continuously reinvented its house codes with their singular aesthetic perspectives. As much as Bottega Veneta is a handbag company, it's also a brand deeply focused on reflecting people's real lives: how they move, feel and dress. And its history reflects just how much a brand so tied to its past can always find itself in the present – no matter the time. *Andiamo.*

THE VENETIAN
SHOP

ROOTED IN VENICE

Bottega Veneta is one of the world's most sought-after luxury
fashion brands today. Both its ready-to-wear offering and
leather goods have disrupted the fashion world over the past
few years, cementing its place in the upper echelons of
the industry, surpassing over €1.5 billion in revenue,
an all-time high for the brand.

A nd it's not only selling – it's gone viral. The brand's
mini Jodie bag, a staple of the house today introduced
by former creative director Daniel Lee, was the most-
searched handbag on the global fashion search platform Lyst
in 2021, seen on the arm of celebrities like Kendall Jenner
and Elsa Hosk, while in 2022, the debut of its current creative
director, Matthieu Blazy, was one of the year's most anticipated
fashion shows.

But Bottega Veneta's Cinderella story didn't happen
overnight. It has taken the brand through the ups and downs of
commercial successes and failures, as well as multiple creative
visions, to materialize in one of modern fashion's biggest booms.

OPPOSITE The Bottega Veneta mini Jodie bag, designed by Daniel Lee,
is one of the brand's most popular items.

ABOVE The Bottega
Veneta showroom
in New York during a
press preview in 1979.

Yet its beginnings can be traced back to something a little more simple. It's all in the name given by its founders, Michele Taddei and Renzo Zengiaro – Bottega Veneta is Italian for "a Venetian shop". Opened in 1966, Bottega Veneta was founded on the idea that impeccable craftsmanship and high-quality materials are the foundation of timeless style. Even after nearly 60 years in business and multiple creative directors and executives at the helm of the ultimate Venetian shop, *Bottega Veneta* stays true to these principles, establishing itself as a symbol of stealth wealth.

But what Michele Taddei and Renzo Zengiaro dreamed in its beginnings had little to do with the Bottega Veneta of today. First opened in Vicenza, Italy, the shop was focused on leather goods, from handbags to luggage. The decision to hone in on accessories rather than ready-to-wear is one of the main reasons for their early success, leading to the creation of their *intrecciato* weaving technique that's become one of the house's signature codes. Legend has it that *intrecciato* was actually born out of necessity. The sewing machines available to Taddei and Zengiaro did not work well with leather materials, so artisans in their shop figured out a way to thread the textiles, resulting in *intrecciato*, an Italian word that translates to "braided".

Unlike other brands at the time, Taddei and Zengiaro decided to forgo logos and monogrammed textiles on their accessories, resulting in a subdued approach to luxury that became a kind of inside secret of the wealthy. Yet, even if the brand didn't achieve mainstream commercial success, the strategy worked: by 1972, Bottega Veneta opened its first shop in New York City, and by 1979, it had boutiques in Los Angeles and Venice. "I've asked myself many times the reason for our success," Vittorio Moltedo, president of Bottega Veneta

BELOW A Bottega Veneta briefcase from the 1970s.

OPPOSITE The
Bottega Veneta
intrecciato handbags
quickly became a
staple for the brand.

Inc., told the *New York Times* in 1979. "I think it's because we have a quality product which we offer in great depth." Even if their handbags were priced between $100 and $450 ($400 to $1,800 in today's value), Bottega Veneta found a clientele willing to pay for their quiet luxury handbags, shoes and luggage: according to Moltedo, in the 1970s, the business had grown from 35 to 50 per cent year over year.

Moltedo's arrival at Bottega Veneta actually marked a before and after for the Italian brand. It all happened in the 1970s, when co-founder Michele Taddei, who was no longer working with Renzo Zengiaro, handed over the company to his ex-wife, Laura Moltedo (neé Braggio), a former personal assistant to Andy Warhol, who brought in her second husband, Vittorio Moltedo, as president of the company. The growth of Bottega Veneta accelerated around this time, with Laura Moltedo as creative director, leading to the opening of 12 stores in the United States.

For clients, the storefronts exemplified the world of simple luxury that Bottega Veneta's founders envisioned for the brand. The Moltedos translated this vision into stores designed by Vittorio Moltedo's brother, an architect based in Rome, who worked with Laura for six months to complete the shops. "It amazes me that they're still talking to each other," Vittorio told the *New York Times.* The result was stores that were divided into four sections – shoes, handbags, luggage and gifts – spread across 370 square metres (4,000 square feet) with velvet shelves installed to showcase handbags.

During the first two decades in business, Bottega Veneta owed its success to its unique approach: contrary to other houses at the time, like Gucci or Louis Vuitton, it offered leather goods that remained logo-free, leaving the *intrecciato* to speak for itself. A photo from *Vogue*'s November 1979 issue, for example, shows a woman opening a brown leather clutch

BELOW A Bottega
Veneta top handle
bag with *intrecciato*
weaving.

featuring the *intrecciato* weave. Shoes went for a similar design: peep-toe sandals and slingback heels also featured the *intrecciato* weaving on one of the brand's magazine ads from the 1970s. Not only were they different from other offerings in the luxury market, but the brand gave clients variety. Handbags were made from textiles like woven leather and printed suede, while shoes came in materials like raffia and two-tone leather. Clients could also forgo the *intrecciato*: for example, the brand made a brown leather briefcase with gold hardware in 1971 that didn't feature the signature weaving. "We have 55 styles of women's bags in 10 colors," Vittorio Moltedo told the *New York Times* in 1979. "If a woman comes in and wants to see a clutch, we can offer her 90 or 50 to choose from."

Things were going well for the young brand. So much so that in the late 1970s, it debuted a new slogan: "When your own initials are enough". Of course, they weren't referring to monogram handbags or large logos, but the "Bottega Veneta" label found inside its leather goods and the *intrecciato* weaving that alerted onlookers when a bag was from Bottega Veneta. Soon, ad campaigns from the brand started featuring this slogan, including a 1978 spread on *Interview* magazine, a marketing strategy that's been upheld until today.

This was all part of Laura and Vittorio Moltedo's plan to convert a once small, struggling shop into a global luxury powerhouse, one that not only grossed in sales but which cemented its role as a mainstay of modern pop culture. The 1980s proved to be the decade when their efforts changed the game for Bottega Veneta. It was only the beginning.

LEFT Handbags were the first core item in Bottega Veneta's business model.

THE ART OF
INTRECCIATO

BOTTEGA VENETA'S SIGNATURE

Bottega Veneta's *intrecciato* has been the defining symbol of the brand since its inception.

It's what's allowed the brand to go logo-free, making its signature technique and leather material the main event, from handbags and shoes to luggage and clothing. For Bottega Veneta creative directors, *intrecciato* has been a playground to evolve the brand's aesthetics beyond the traditional weaving.

Throughout its 60-year history, *intrecciato* has kept Bottega Veneta afloat. As other luxury brands have constantly tuned their approach to logomania to match the social and economic landscape, Bottega Veneta has remained true to its philosophy that craftsmanship is king. So much so that the *New York Times'* reporter Ruth La Ferla once described it as "subtle, long-lasting, and recession-proof." But that doesn't mean *intrecciato* has remained the same. It's actually shifted with the times, too.

OPPOSITE A pair of sunglasses from Tomas Maier's era at Bottega Veneta, mimicking the look of *intrecciato* weaving.

ABOVE The *intrecciato* weaving has been reinterpreted by Bottega Veneta designers since its inception in the 1960s.

Today, Bottega Veneta's *intrecciato* handbags are handmade at the house's atelier outside of the province of Vicenza, located inside a renovated eighteenth-century villa, which holds 300 employees. But, back in the 1960s, *intrecciato* was borne out of necessity to match the tools available in the Veneto region of Italy, where the brand was founded. While the area had a strong legacy of clothing manufacturing, leather goods and accessories were a novelty. In turn, the sewing machines available were too weak to work with leather, leading artisans at Bottega Veneta to look for alternatives. They settled on using finer leather that could be put under the needles available at the time. By sacrificing thickness, artisans realized that they could make the leather stronger by braiding the leather threads by hand. That's how Bottega Veneta

artisans were able to make a metallic clutch in 1966 – now found in the collection at the Museum at FIT, New York – for example, or peep-toe shoes that featured the woven detail throughout.

Over time, creative directors at Bottega Veneta have pushed the boundaries of *intrecciato*, while staying true to its heritage and finding commercial success in the process. Take, for example, the Cabat bag, a sizable tote bag that features a rectangular shape with *intrecciato* weaving panels. With no logos or flashy details, the bag retailed for $2,800 to $4,500 in 2001 when first introduced in 2001 under creative director Tomas Maier – and today, it's still one of the most sought-after handbags from Bottega Veneta, retailing from $5,000 for a mini version to $15,000 for a large one.

ABOVE An *intrecciato* weave bag from Bottega Veneta made of raffia.

It might seem ludicrous that a bag so simple could be worth so much, but the *intrecciato* is precisely what has allowed Bottega Veneta to charge about a month's rent for a handbag. Each piece takes about two days to make. In comparison, a standard luxury bag takes about two hours, according to the *New York Times*. *Intrecciato*'s qualities, therefore, invite clients to pay for luxury materials – not logos – that are durable and expensive.

OPPOSITE Designers have included *intrecciato* references in clothing too through prints, embellishments and threading.

LEFT A Bottega Veneta Knot bag from the Spring/Summer 2016 collection.

Another clear example is the Knot bag, one of Bottega Veneta's most popular bags. The rectangular curvy clutch, which features a metal knot closure, was first introduced by Maier in 2002, and has since been reintroduced by current creative director Matthieu Blazy, retailing for over $3,000 in 2023. Throughout its 20-year history, the Knot has been Bottega Veneta's official red carpet handbag, seen on celebrities like Nicole Kidman, Sarah Jessica Parker, Sandra Bullock, Zoe Saldaña, Kim Kardashian, Rosario Dawson and Mila Kunis. So much so that from the early 2000s until the late 2010s, it was hard to look at a red carpet, including the Academy Awards and Golden Globe Awards, without seeing the Knot bag on the hand of a celebrity. It's also featured on special moments for many celebrities: Sandra Bullock, for example, wore a plum Knot bag on the night she won a Golden Globe award for *The Blind Side* in 2010, while Edie Falco sported a black version for the 62nd Annual Primetime Emmy Awards ceremony that same year, when she took home a statue for *Nurse Jackie*. Without any logos, the Knot bag was distinguishable only by its shape and, of course, the *intrecciato*. It's one of the best exemplifications of Bottega Veneta's "if you know, you know" approach to fashion and accessories.

As a leather goods brand, Bottega Veneta has mostly embedded *intrecciato* on handbags, luggage and shoes. But designers have also incorporated it into clothing. For example, Laura Moltedo and former designer Edward Buchanan included an *intrecciato* scarf and skirt in the Autumn 2000 collection, braiding cashmere and leather, while former creative director Giles Deacon showed a yellow moto jacket for the brand's Autumn/Winter 2001 collection made from *intrecciato*. Maier also put *intrecciato* on jackets constantly, including a Spring 2006 brown belted leather jacket that was paired with a Cabat bag. Former creative director Daniel Lee also embedded

intrecciato into clothing. In the Autumn 2019 lineup – his debut at the Italian house – Lee included a brown coat made from *intrecciato*; later, for Spring 2020, the designer included a pale blue pencil skirt made from a leather weaving similar to *intrecciato*; and finally, for the Spring 2022 collection, he reworked *intrecciato* into knitwear pieces.

But the viral success of Bottega Veneta in the last five years has shown that it's the brand's *intrecciato* handbags that truly make it a commercial triumph. Handbags like the Cassette bag, a rectangular purse that features a thicker leather braiding, and the Jodie, a tote bag that displays *intrecciato* weaving from the panels to the handle and is tied with a heavy knot, made the Italian house one of the most successful in fashion in the 2020s. Not only in value – after Daniel Lee took over, the brand grew its revenue from $1.5 billion to nearly $4 billion – but also in mainstream popularity, seen on the hand of powerful influencers like Alexandra Pereira and Chiara Ferragni on street style photographs and social media. With no logos to bear, it was the *intrecciato* that won over a new generation once again.

A new lineup of *intrecciato* handbags continues that legacy under creative director Matthieu Blazy, who is focusing on this category because, as he told *Vogue* in 2022, he feels "Bottega Veneta is a bag company." In his debut collection for Autumn 2022, Blazy introduced the Sardine bag, a curved bag similar to the Jodie that features a hardware handle made from *intrecciato*, that's been worn by celebrities like Kendall Jenner and Rosie Huntington-Whiteley. Later, for Spring 2023, the designer showed the *Andiamo* bag, a 2020s version of the Cabat tote bag. Much as its name suggests – *Andiamo* means "let's go" in Italian – the bag is a roomy top handle design that also features an *intrecciato* shoulder handle and gold hardware. *Marie Claire* style director Sara Holzman reviewed the handbag, concluding: "The bag was super easy to have by my side while traipsing through

OPPOSITE The *intrecciato* weaving was a signature of Daniel Lee's tenure at Bottega Veneta, using the traditional weaving with bold colours.

OVERLEAF Handbags displayed at Bottega Veneta stores in 2014.

OPPOSITE The
Sardine bag by
Bottega Veneta
debuted in Autumn
2022, under
creative director
Matthieu Blazy.

crowds, cars, and crowded cafés." Similarly to Maier's Cabat bag, the Andiamo is *intrecciato* made to be on the go.

While handbags continue to be Bottega Veneta's hero product, shoes have also been a strong category for the brand to flex its *intrecciato* muscles. Most recently, Blazy introduced the Canalazzo boot, an over-the-knee boot made in both regular and *intrecciato* leather, in the Autumn 2022 and Spring 2023 collections. But his predecessor, Daniel Lee, was specially gifted in making *intrecciato* footwear a main focus for the brand. The Lido mule, for example, a square-toe sandal that featured an *intrecciato* strap, became one of the most recognizable accessories during Lee's tenure, while his padded texture, which mimicked *intrecciato* without the traditional weaving, was also featured on a variety of mules, sandals and pumps.

The success of Lee and Blazy's *intrecciato* footwear at Bottega Veneta was built on the strong legacy left by Tomas Maier, who, throughout his 17-year-run at the brand, focused heavily on making shoes a defining category for the house, alongside handbags. Maier started introducing *intrecciato* footwear in the brand's Spring 2005 collection with a pair of slingback flats, which later evolved into pieces like *intrecciato* slingback pumps with fringe detailing for Autumn 2005, country club-ready wedges with a platform made from *intrecciato* for Spring 2008 and sock-like knee-high boots with *intrecciato* details on the toes for Autumn 2015.

Intrecciato may have been borne out of a lack of resources but what Bottega Veneta artisans birthed became the logo to end all logos, a symbol that's been reworked by designers over time. Each one's singular vision for Bottega Veneta has transformed a weaving technique into embellishments and even *trompe l'oeil* details that have also proven commercially successful. Necessity truly is the mother of invention.

READY-TO-WEAR, TAKE ONE

BOTTEGA VENETA TAKES THE RUNWAY

By the late 1970s and 1980s, Vittorio and Laura Moltedo had made Bottega Veneta a booming luxury goods business. Its accessories and handbags were sought-after by the ultra elite and celebrities, soon becoming a pop culture phenomenon too.

I n 1978, for example, Moltedo joined forces with her former boss Andy Warhol to publish a two-page ad in *Interview* magazine's December issue, which featured model Bianca Jagger on the cover. Later, in 1980, actor and model Lauren Hutton carried a Bottega Veneta handbag in the movie *American Gigolo*. And in 1985, Andy Warhol released *Bottega Veneta Industrial Videotape*, a short film made for the Italian house with music by Madonna that showed everything from the brand's artisanal craftsmanship to its American stores.

With a booming accessories business, it was only a matter of time before the Moltedos started thinking about Bottega Veneta's expansion into the world of ready-to-wear. Following

OPPOSITE A look from the Bottega Veneta Autumn/Winter 1999 collection, designed by Laura Moltedo and Edward Buchanan.

OPPOSITE A look
from the Bottega
Veneta Autumn/
Winter 1999
collection, designed
by Laura Moltedo and
Edward Buchanan.

BELOW The fall 1999
collection by Bottega
Veneta showed a
minimalist aesthetic
in a sober palette.

the example of brands like Fendi, which had successfully
transformed its family-owned fur and handbags workshop into
a ready-to-wear line designed by Karl Lagerfeld, the Moltedos
sought to transition the brand into a new category, keeping the
leather goods as the pillar. Laura Moltedo took over creative
direction for Bottega Veneta, and in 1995, she was joined by
a 26-year-old recent graduate from Parsons School of Design:
Edward Buchanan. His first task was to develop the first-ever
Bottega Veneta ready-to-wear collection as design director.
"I was very green," he later told the *New York Times*. Bottega
Veneta's first fashion show was staged three years later at
Palazzo Serbelloni in Milan.

Over the next few years, Moltedo and Buchanan slowly
established the foundations of the brand's clothing identity.
Much like its handbags, Bottega Veneta's clothes needed to

BOTTEG

RIGHT AND OPPOSITE Rich chocolate and delicate white hues were the predominant colours in the fall 1999 collection.

speak volumes without making too much noise, resulting in minimalist takes on everyday essentials that served as a canvas for the brand's accessories to shine. Take, for example, the Autumn 1999 collection, which included a mostly black, white and cream palette with long coats, maxi hemlines and crisp shirts across the lineup, while the Spring 2000 collection, which *Vogue* described as "a line of simple, easygoing separates", featured more pops of colour with pieces in lime green and coral.

Buchanan's run at Bottega Veneta was defined by more than his design direction. While the brand had mainstream and pop culture success, it had long served a white elite clientele and Buchanan, a Black man from Ohio, wanted to change this. At the time, stylists were telling him that it was hard to get luxury fashion houses to dress their clients, who were mostly in the R&B and hip-hop scene. So, Buchanan opened the doors for many of them to wear Bottega Veneta. He famously dressed R&B singer Lauryn Hill, including a pair of boots and sunglasses she sported at the 1999 MTV Video Music Awards. "Many companies weren't giving clothing to hip-hop and R&B stars because they weren't considered a valid reflection of existing consumers. I attempted to stomp that theory out," he explained to the *New York Times*. "I was fortunate because I had a high level of support and security on the inside."

After a fruitful six years, Buchanan exited the company to launch his own label, leaving Bottega Veneta and the Moltedos searching for a new designer.

They settled on Central Saint Martins alumnus Giles Deacon, a UK-born creative who had previous experience working for designer Jean-Charles de Castelbajac. Entering his first creative director role, Deacon had no easy task: although Laura Moltedo and Edward Buchanan had established a strong visual identity for Bottega Veneta's ready-to-wear collections, it

LEFT British designer Giles Deacon took over Bottega Veneta's creative direction in 2000.

OPPOSITE A look from Deacon's debut collection for Bottega Veneta.

was still outshone by its accessories. The brand needed a press and retail boost that would bring back its pop culture status. "The brief that we were given was to kind of really go wild and do some really exciting shows that would bring in a lot of press attention," Deacon later told SHOWstudio.

Moltedo also hired stylist Katie Grand to help develop the next vision for Bottega Veneta. Grand, a British journalist and stylist, had worked at *POP* and *Dazed & Confused*, and was serving as fashion director of *The Face* in 2000. In hiring Grand, Moltedo was bringing in youth culture and indie sensibility that had not been seen at Bottega Veneta – yet.

RIGHT AND OPPOSITE Giles Deacon disrupted Bottega Veneta with bright colours and modern styles, a departure for the otherwise classic and minimalist brand.

For the Autumn 2001 collection, Deacon and Grand, alongside accessories designer Stuart Vevers, reimagined the brand's ready-to-wear for the 2000s, incorporating some of the key elements of Y2K fashion: logos, bright colours and miniskirts. "Bottega Veneta is undergoing a major face-lift that could lead to a completely new identity," read a *Vogue* review about the collection. But there were still some heritage details in the lineup: although the colour palette seemed unorthodox for Bottega Veneta, it was parallel to the hues found in the shoes back in the 1970s and 1980s, including the signature "Bottega green", one of the brand's biggest signifiers today. There were also pieces made from *intrecciato*, including leather jackets, as well as large briefcases referenced in Bret Easton Ellis's *American Psycho*.

The group accomplished their task: the collection received major press coverage. But the new vision was ultimately not the right one for the brand. In February 2001, the luxury fashion conglomerate Gucci Group – now, Kering – bought a 66 per cent stake in Bottega Veneta, and later, in July of that year, acquired an additional 11 per cent, gaining control of the company. The Moltedos exited the company shortly after.

For all the tumult of the period, this was the era when Bottega Veneta was able to sculpt itself into the brand it is today, mostly by figuring out what it's not. Logomania, for example, which Deacon included in his Autumn 2001 collection, is one of the main sartorial practices the house has kept at bay over the years. This period also allowed the brand to earn mainstream recognition via celebrity endorsements and strategic marketing – something that it would later bank on. And, while the Moltedos eventually gave away control of the company, their creative and business risks turned Bottega Veneta into a global brand.

What they did set up all that follows.

OPPOSITE The Autumn/Winter 2001 collection by Giles Deacon marked the first time Bottega Veneta included logos in their lineup.

READY-TO-WEAR,
TAKE TWO

WELCOME, TOMAS MAIER

When the Gucci Group, an affiliate of the company Pinault-Printemps-Redoute, bought Bottega Veneta in 2001 for $56 million, the brand was undergoing financial difficulties.

T he year before, Bottega Veneta had an annual revenue of $50 million, a low number in the world of luxury goods. But businessman Domenico De Sole and designer Tom Ford, who spearheaded the acquisition, believed in the brand's heritage and its potential for mass success. All they needed to find was the right person to guide the brand's vision.

The German designer Tomas Maier turned out to be the right name for the job. With previous freelance stints at Hèrmes and Sonia Rykiel, Maier was familiar with the world of luxury goods. "Taste and toil have been the touchstones of his until-now low-profile career," wrote *Vogue*'s Sally Singer of Maier. But he was far from the likely choice. A previous freelancer with no creative director role under his belt, Maier had known Tom

OPPOSITE Tomas Maier backstage at his inaugural presentation for Bottega Veneta in 2004.

OVERLEAF Models at Maier's debut presentation for Bottega Veneta.

ABOVE Models backstage at the inaugural presentation for Tomas Maier at Bottega Veneta.

OPPOSITE Actor Sarah Jessica Parker and Tomas Maier at the Bottega Veneta flagship store opening on September 2004 in New York City.

Ford since the 1980s, but when he was approached about the possibility of taking over the top job at Bottega Veneta he was based in Miami, growing his own eponymous label focusing on swimwear. Yet, the unorthodox pick was the only name Ford was interested in to lead the creative direction of the Italian house. Still, Maier had some reservations about the role, asking Ford to be allowed to visit the Vicenza workshop to see for himself the brand's artisanal process. He also wanted Gucci Group to allow him to continue developing his own label and to take over the creative control of all things Bottega Veneta, including advertising. Ford and Gucci Group agreed, and so, in June 2021, the company named Maier as creative director of Bottega Veneta, an appointment that would define the history of the Italian house.

Maier had his work cut out for him. Bottega Veneta's ready-to-wear collections had been cut by Gucci Group, scaling

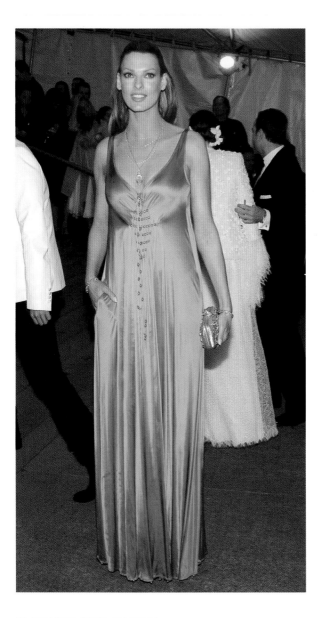

back the business to only accessories and leather goods – its origins. Any other designer might have struggled with the idea of starting from scratch, but Maier – adept at the stealth wealth sensibility and intensely meticulous – dived right in.

It didn't matter to Maier that the fashion industry was ruled by logomania and overt excess brought on by the Y2K period. Think corsets, low-rise pants, mixed prints, chain belts and buzzy "It" bags that included the *Sex and the City*-endorsed Fendi Baguette. Maier had no interest in fitting in with that culture. Instead, he wanted to raise Bottega Veneta's quality and design to a level that would make it impossible for the fashion industry *and* the public to ignore. "The 'It' Bag is a totally marketed bullshit crap," Maier told the *New Yorker* in 2011. "I don't believe that's how you make something that's lasting—that becomes iconic as a design."

Still, Maier focused on building a hero handbag that would encompass Bottega Veneta's design and lifestyle philosophies. He settled on the Cabat bag, a roomy tote with two handles and no logos, which was revealed to the public in September 2001. Retailing at a whopping $6,000 and featuring none of the standard qualities of an "It" bag of the 2000s, Maier's Cabat stood alone in the accessories landscape. But his commitment to the handbag persisted: instead of retiring the bag after a few months, like other brands did, the Cabat would be shown every season and sold only at Bottega Veneta stores. It also deviated from the standard weaving methods artisans used to make the *intrecciato*. Maier wanted the Cabat to have an even more artisanal feel, substituting the cotton backing and base panel found in previous Bottega Veneta bags for hand-braided double-sided leather. And so, the simple yet complicated tote bag became synonymous with Bottega Veneta, and vice versa. As Tom Ford said of Maier's move, "By not doing the 'It' Bag, you do the 'It' Bag."

OPPOSITE
Supermodel Linda Evangelista attends the Met Gala wearing Bottega Veneta in 2005.

OVERLEAF A Bottega Veneta Knot bag.

RIGHT Tomas Maier and film-maker Liz Goldwyn at the Met Gala in 2006.

After years of turbulence at Bottega Veneta, it was becoming clear that Maier's mission was to go back to the brand's motto: "When your own initials are enough". But also to reach a type of customer who, as the *New Yorker* described in 2011, "disdains the easy status recognition that comes from a conspicuous logo."

Although Maier was now the de facto face of one of fashion's most well-known brands, he thought of himself an outsider. Born in Germany's Black Forest and growing up as the son of an architect, he had no fashion pedigree and didn't live amid the metropolitan flashiness where the industry often booms. To pursue his fashion dreams, Maier enrolled at the

École de la Chambre Syndicale de la Couture Parisienne, under the aegis of La Chambre Syndicale de la Haute Couture, the storied institution that regulates and preserves French fashion. In doing so, he was following in the footsteps of other designers like Karl Lagerfeld, Yves Saint Laurent, Valentino and Issey Miyake. Even when Maier entered the fashion world, he did so behind the scenes, working on leather goods and accessories at Hermès and designing menswear at Sonia Rykiel. Before then, he had contemplated a career as an architect. But by 2001, Maier was under a spotlight as he tried to salvage an Italian house with less than 50 workshop employees and looming bankruptcy.

During the first few years, the designer focused solely on leather goods and accessories, much as the Bottega Veneta founders did in the early days. Although the Cabat

LEFT Tomas Maier's Cabat bag was his first hit for Bottega Veneta.

bag was earning the brand recognition and revenue – by 2004 Bottega Veneta was completely profitable – Maier ultimately decided it was time for Bottega Veneta to get back on the ready-to-wear game again. It would debut in the spring of 2004.

For his first lineup, Maier unveiled 60 looks for an Autumn/Winter 2005 collection, which he said wasn't regular ready-to-wear. "I had the concept of designing clothes like accessories. Everyone has their own personality, and will pick things out to wear in their own way," he told *Vogue*'s Sarah Mower, who described the collection as "feminine and modern". From tweed A-line skirts and colourful tights to flower printed dresses, the collection embodied some of the playful aspects from Giles Deacon's era at Bottega Veneta but stayed true to Maier's clean and minimal aesthetic, while for the accessories, he drew inspiration from the 1960s, reissuing a croc handbag from that decade.

Throughout the late 2000s, Maier continued with a similar strategy at Bottega Veneta, always prioritizing functionality and quality. And as creative director, who also dipped into advertising and marketing, he also sought to bring Bottega Veneta some of the celebrity cachet it had in the past. Understanding the power of mainstream approval, Maier was seen with names like Sarah Jessica Parker, who attended the opening of a Bottega Veneta New York City store in 2004. Parker has proved to be an influencer in the world of luxury goods: years prior, when her *Sex and the City* character Carrie Bradshaw sported the Fendi Baguette bag and the Dior Saddle bag, the popularity of the two models exploded. So here was Parker in the mid-2000s, carrying a Bottega Veneta Knot bag, first released in 2002, on her arm. The It girl carried the not-so-It bag.

OPPOSITE Sarah Jessica Parker at the 2006 Golden Globes, carrying a Bottega Veneta Knot bag.

74 READY-TO-WEAR, TAKE TWO

RIGHT Penélope Cruz attends the premiere of the film *Broken Embraces* in 2009 wearing Bottega Veneta.

OPPOSITE A leather trench coat look from the Bottega Veneta Autumn/Winter 2009 collection.

OPPOSITE Sandra
Bullock wearing a
Bottega Veneta dress
at the 2010 Golden
Globe Awards.

OVERLEAF Bottega
Veneta Knot
handbags.

Other celebrities started carrying Bottega Veneta handbags at red carpet and social events around that time. Scarlett Johansson sported a metallic Knot bag at the Academy Awards in 2004, while Marisa Tomei donned a pink version for the premiere of the film *Alfie* in the same year. Nicole Kidman, Penélope Cruz, Linda Evangelista, Rosario Dawson and Kim Kardashian were some of the names that soon jumped on the craze for Bottega Veneta Knot bags.

As Maier expanded the brand, he also began thinking about continuing Bottega Veneta's craftsmanship for generations to come. In an industrialized world, Bottega Veneta's artisanal process is a dying art, but Maier thought of a way to keep it moving, and in 2006, the brand opened La Scuola dei Maestri Pellettieri di Bottega Veneta in partnership with the Università Iuav di Venezia in Vicenza, Italy, for students to learn traditional manufacturing, construction and, of course, its signature *intrecciato* weaving.

The 2000s also proved to be a time of geographical expansion for Bottega Veneta. Its biggest store at the time opened its doors in Tokyo in 2007, spanning five floors and 900 square metres (9,700 square feet), with offices and a showroom occupying the top floors. That same year, the brand opened nine other stores, including its biggest European flagship at the time in Rome, a display of its success amid a time of economic recession. But Maier trusted his stealth wealth designs enough to understand that, when consumers don't want flashy products, a brand like Bottega Veneta is set to prevail, despite its sky-high prices.

On the runway, the collections were proving successful for Maier. Sticking with a minimalist design mindset, he often stayed within a limited colour palette – going lighter in the spring and darker in the autumn – and showed a preference for sleek silhouettes and wardrobe staples, like shirt dresses

and leather coats, that didn't exude flashiness beyond their hefty price tags. *Vogue*'s Sarah Mower described his shows in the mid-to-late 2000s as "a stripped-down statement" and stated that "the clothes are now vying with the accessories for attention in this luxury house."

This became clear in the 2010s, when Bottega Veneta's designs evolved from stealth wealth essentials into red carpet-ready gowns. For the Spring 2009 collection, Maier unveiled a series of white and cream dresses that showed a departure from the brand's tried-and-true model of everyday clothes, and later, for the spring 2010 collection, he continued it with three strapless flowing dresses in black, orange and purple. They quickly appeared on the red carpet: *Gossip Girl* star Leighton Meester wore a white gown with knotted sleeves from the Spring 2009 collection to the Primetime Emmy Awards in 2009, while Sandra Bullock sported a plum Spring 2010 gown to accept her Golden Globe Award in 2010.

It was a sign that Bottega Veneta's leading man was experimenting outside of the brand's comfort zone with success. And the numbers showed it too. By 2012, a decade after Maier's start at Bottega Veneta, the brand surpassed $1 billion in revenue for the first time in its history. In 2013, 12 years after Maier joining Bottega Veneta, the company became part of the Kering Group, the luxury company formed by Pinault-Printemps-Redoute, joining other iconic houses like Balenciaga, Brioni and Alexander McQueen.

Since Bottega Veneta crossed the billion-dollar threshold, Maier worked arduously to secure his legacy at the brand, from his ready-to-wear designs to the creative efforts behind the scenes, celebrating both his own work and the collaborators that made it possible. One area he specifically focused on was advertising. Back in 2001, when he took over the reins at Bottega Veneta, Maier was adamant about

OPPOSITE Leighton Meester attends the 2009 Primetime Emmy Awards wearing a gown by Bottega Veneta.

RIGHT A look from the Bottega Veneta Spring/Summer 2011 collection.

OPPOSITE A menswear Bottega Veneta look from the Spring/Summer 2012 collection.

LEFT Fringe, as seen in this look from the Spring/Summer 2013 collection, became a signature style of Bottega Veneta.

OPPOSITE Tomas Maier's collections presented a wide variety of Knot bags, as seen in this look from the Autumn/Winter 2016 collection.

OVERLEAF A lineup of looks from the Bottega Veneta Spring/Summer 2013 collection.

having full creative control over anything related to the brand, including its visual aesthetics. He took advantage of this opportunity to establish a conceptual universe for Bottega Veneta's ads, which were rooted in collaborations with photographers like Annie Leibovitz and Peter Lindbergh. In 2015, he published *Bottega Veneta: Art of Collaboration*, a compilation of the brand's ad campaigns with a foreword by journalist Tim Blanks. "It may sound odd to compile a book of ads, but for Bottega Veneta, campaigns are somewhat of an art form," read a review in *New York Magazine*.

Art of Collaboration was not only a survey of Bottega Veneta's ad campaigns from 2002 to 2016, but a look inside Maier's mind as a creative beyond the runway. In the book, he described shooting an ad with photographer Nan Goldin at an old house in Staten Island in 2010 and at the New York Botanical Garden in the Bronx for a 2014 campaign. While Maier showed a strong control over creative materials at Bottega Veneta, he allowed artists and photographers to fulfil their own visions. "When I have such a huge amount of respect for what they do, how could the outcome go wrong?" he told Artnet in 2015.

Under Tomas Maier, Bottega Veneta had effectively quieted the possibilities of bankruptcy that had erupted at the turn of the century. The designer had fulfilled the vision of the brand's founders, establishing a successful leather goods business and expanding it into a ready-to-wear success that was rapidly taking over the fashion industry. It had impressed critics and celebrities, cementing Bottega Veneta as a brand that was uniquely positioned for further success in the decades to come.

Maier had also grown his own persona over this period. As he managed to live between Florida and Italy, overseeing both Bottega Veneta and his eponymous label, he became one of fashion's most buzzed about designers. In 2016, he

OPPOSITE A look from the Bottega Veneta Autumn/ Winter 2018 collection, worn by Irina Shayk.

celebrated 15 years at Bottega Veneta, just as the brand reached its 50th anniversary. "I am honoured to have led our story, and to have the opportunity to continue leading it," he told *British Vogue* that year.

So, when Tomas Maier decided to exit Bottega Veneta after 17 years at the helm, the announcement shocked the industry. "It's largely due to Tomas's high-level creative demands that Bottega Veneta became the house it is today. He put it back on the luxury scene and made it an undisputed reference," a statement from Kering, Bottega Veneta's parent company, chairman and CEO François-Henri Pinault read. It was hard to imagine why Maier would leave the brand he'd spent nearly two decades building (Kering never commented on the reasons for his departure), but clearly this was the end of an era.

OPPOSITE A handbag featuring *intrecciato* detailing from the Bottega Veneta Autumn/Winter 2017 collection.

BELOW Models at Tomas Maier's debut presentation for Bottega Veneta.

OVERLEAF Designer Tomas Maier transformed Bottega Veneta from a leather goods business into an international brand.

THE
LONG-AWAITED
BOOM

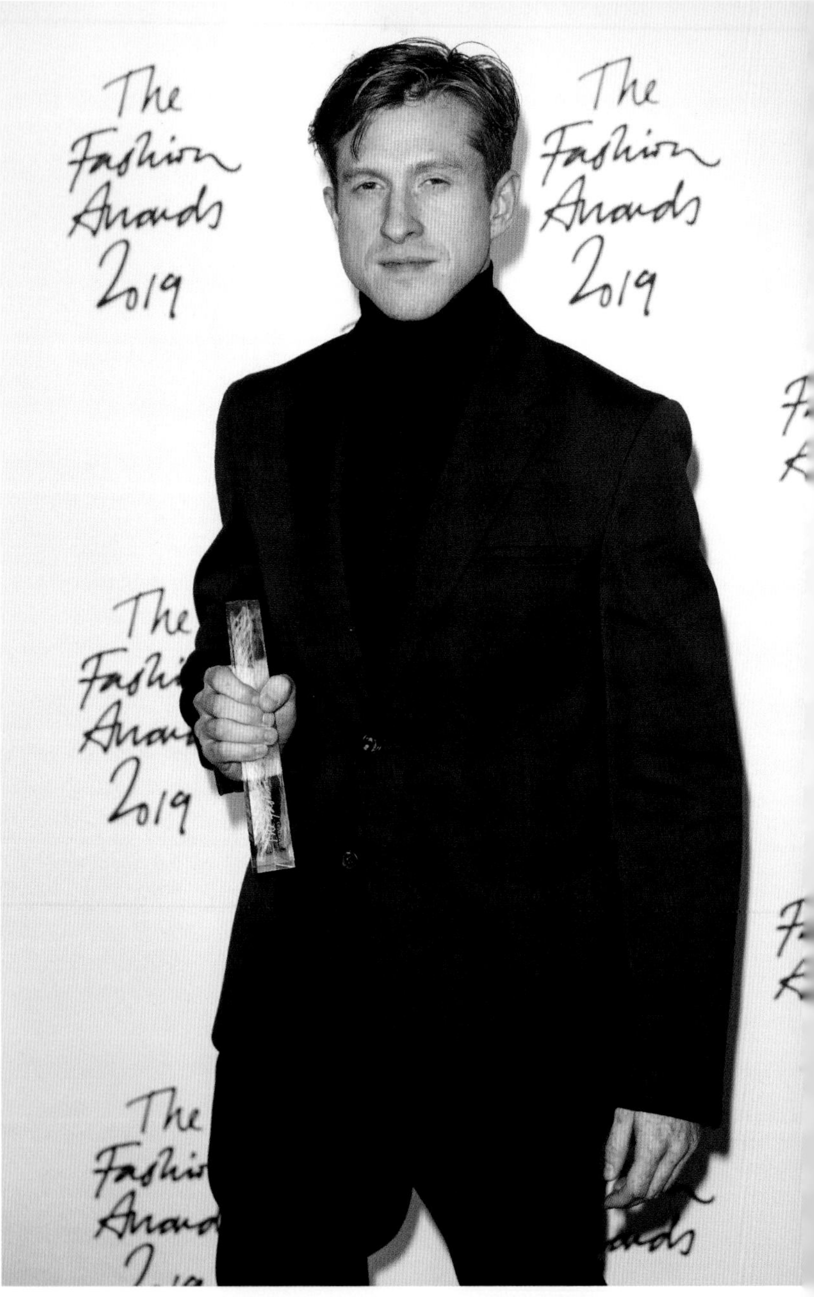

THE DANIEL LEE ERA BEGINS

In the nearly 20 years that Tomas Maier led the house of Bottega Veneta, its success skyrocketed, cementing a solid client base for its ready-to-wear and leather goods, as well as furthering its *intrecciato* and craftsmanship legacy. But towards the latter end of his creative directorship, the fashion industry wondered if it was time for Maier to step down.

Sales at the company had dwindled: its revenue fell by 9 per cent between 2016 and 2017, falling to €1.2 billion. Amid that slippage, the brand opened its largest ever store on Madison Avenue, sprawling five floors and half a block and taking over three nineteenth-century townhouses. It also moved its catwalk show from Milan to New York. Ultimately, the stealth wealth strategy of Tomas Maier's Bottega Veneta failed to become the kind of pop culture phenomenon other brands, including Alessandro Michele's Gucci, had achieved around that era. It was not enough to feed the *if you know, you know* mentality anymore.

So, in June 2018, Kering announced that Maier would be exiting the company. Minimal details were given around his

OPPOSITE Designer Daniel Lee at the 2019 Fashion Awards in London.

ABOVE A handbag from the Bottega Veneta Pre-Fall 2019 collection, the first from Daniel Lee.

departure and Maier moved on to work on his eponymous label. But just two days later, Kering announced a replacement: Daniel Lee.

"Daniel Lee has a deep understanding of the house's current challenges both in terms of creation and development," said Claus-Dietrich Lahrs, chief executive of Bottega Veneta at the time of Lee's appointment. "He will bring to Bottega Veneta a new and distinctive creative language."

A graduate of Central Saint Martins and former alum of Phoebe Philo's Céline, Lee was relatively unknown at the time, much like Maier before he entered Bottega Veneta. "No one knew who I was before this job, which is quite nice," he told British *Vogue* in 2019. "Bottega is about discretion and ultimate sophistication; it's elusive, a little bit insider, a little bit coded, all those things I really like." A behind-the-scenes designer, who didn't have a public Instagram account, Lee had been a fashion insider's secret. Yet, he was hardly the only obscure name being appointed to the highest of jobs in fashion during that time: Gucci, which is also owned by Kering, had hired Alessandro Michele in 2015, who then transformed the brand into a global phenomenon. In hiring Lee, Kering was clearly wanting to test this strategy with Bottega Veneta.

But Lee's appointment also had a lot to do with his experience at Phoebe Philo's Céline. The designer had established a loyal clientele of minimalist fans who were not interested in gimmicks, developing a cult following that was abruptly surprised when Philo exited Céline in 2017. Yet, Maier's Bottega Veneta did not fill that void, and Lee, who

BELOW A pair of padded pumps by Daniel Lee's Bottega Veneta.

had helped in Philo's success as design director and worked at houses like Balenciaga, Maison Margiela and Donna Karan, was equipped to do it.

With the appointment, Bottega Veneta was also making a statement about its future. At the time, 85 per cent of the sales were leather goods, a category that had been the brand's bread and butter since its founding. But even with Lee's pedigree, he was more adept at ready-to-wear than leather goods. His hiring signalled that the company was betting on the British designer to deliver its long-awaited ready-to-wear boom.

"I look forward to evolving what has gone before, while contributing a new perspective and modernity," Lee said in a press release announcing his appointment, which began in July 2018. A few months later, he debuted his first collection. The changes were monumental.

Early on, the brand announced it would move away from the Milan Fashion Week slot, opting for off-season collections in salon-style shows that would rotate cities across the world. As he started to work at Bottega Veneta, Lee also opted to keep the artisans who had laboured at the brand for decades. (He also transformed the corporate gym into the atelier and a photo studio into his design studio.) But knowing the brand's ready-to-wear lacked the oomph he craved, Lee replaced part of the design team, bringing in new hires. One of them was Daisy Butler, a former classmate at Central Saint Martins, who worked as head of heritage at Bottega Veneta. "She understands me," Lee told *Cultured* in 2020. "We inspire each other and build the ideas together over countless conversations. It's so crucial to have that back-and-forth." Ultimately, the decision to bring in familiar faces stemmed from Lee's approach to having co-workers that feel like a community. "I love the way that [fashion] brings people together, how it connects people from different parts of the world," he told British *Vogue*. "You

LEFT The Cassette handbag, first introduced in the Autumn/Winter 2019 collection, became one of Bottega Veneta's biggest-selling bags.

OPPOSITE Daniel Lee introduced the triangle closure in his debut collection.

can be rich or poor, talent will always rise to the surface in this industry. It's a level playing field."

For the pre-fall 2019 lineup – his first showing for the brand – Lee began introducing motifs that became signature of his time at Bottega Veneta: relaxed styles and bright colours sprinkled across a collection of everyday wears that fit seemingly in every customer's wardrobe. "I like real clothes. I think there's a need for a return to elegance and sophistication," he told *Vogue* about the collection. And, of course, he reintroduced *intrecciato* with his own twist, including a leather skirt and supersized bags with oversized braiding, as well as quilted textures that resembled the signature technique. "With a little bit of thinking you can do so much with the weave. I liked the idea of enlarging it because I like things that are bold and quite direct," he told British *Vogue*. And while the brand long rejected logos, Lee introduced a triangle-shaped metal closure that soon became a house signature, and which has remained a part of the collections since.

Lee also rebooted the brand's presence on social media, especially Instagram, and presented the Pre-Fall 2019 lookbook in a white cube format with flash photography. It was a departure from Maier's creative approach, which prioritized an editorial style, dramatic sensitivity in ad campaigns. For the Spring 2019 campaign, Lee's Bottega Veneta hired photographer Tyrone Lebon – a British fashion photographer who also works with brands like Miu Miu, Calvin Klein and Louis Vuitton – and art director Edward Quarmby – a strategist for film, print, spatial and product design. The result was a series of images that put models and their relaxed wears at the forefront, with classic leather trenches and white tank tops heavily featured.

But Lee's catwalk debut came that winter when he showed the house's Autumn/Winter 2019 collection at Parco Sempione

OPPOSITE Actor Salma Hayek exits a Bottega Veneta show carrying a Pouch bag.

during Milan Fashion Week, collaborating with stylist Marie Chaix, who had previously worked for Philo, Proenza Schouler and The Row. The *New York Times*' critic Vanessa Friedman described the lineup as "clearly in the vernacular of Old Céline", referring to the colloquial name given to Philo's era, and "an impressively confident and coherent debut". Lee, who was only 32 years old, was navigating high expectations from an industry that was looking for the kind of cool, wearable clothing that other brands were forgoing. And he delivered.

Changing the visual aesthetic at Bottega Veneta didn't bother him. It also didn't matter to Lee if the brand lost loyal customers because of this new creative approach. "Bottega Veneta is a company built on woven handbags – and, well, we still have those woven handbags," he told British *Vogue*. "What was so fantastic [about taking on this role] is that I wasn't so scared about losing our ready-to-wear, shoes and jewellery customers as it was such a small part of the business by comparison, and that gives you a certain confidence to tear things up." It was this security in his design sensibility that ultimately earned Bottega Veneta a mainstream following that had been hard for other creative directors to attain. Lee's Bottega Veneta was bringing the brand's heritage into pop culture like never before.

And amassing diehard fans. Soon after his debut, in July 2019, a new Instagram account with the handle @newbottega emerged, chronicling the rapid changes and cult following that Daniel Lee's Bottega Veneta was generating. In its square tiles, fashion fans could see some of Lee's biggest hits: the square-toed *intrecciato* quilted mules and the Padded Cassette handbag that became signature codes for his tenure. It was a similar phenomenon to the @oldceline Instagram account that was launched after Phoebe Philo's departure, when the brand deleted traces of her work from their social media, replacing it

OPPOSITE A model wearing the Maxi Jodie bag during the Bottega Veneta Spring/Summer 2020 catwalk.

with the vision of the new creative director, Hedi Slimane. But @newbottega looked forward instead, confirming that Kering's strategy to bring in a Philo-adjacent name to focus on more wearable codes for Bottega Veneta was working.

With a strong following emerging, Lee flexed his creative muscles even further for the Spring 2020 show, especially in the accessories department. In that collection, he introduced the Pouch, a voluminous half-moon clutch that looked similar to a Bottega Veneta bag worn by Lauren Hutton in the 1980 film *American Gigolo*. But Lee, who was looking to establish himself as an accessories designer, reworked the handbag, introducing a thick gold chain that transformed the clutch into a shoulder bag and forgoing the *intrecciato* braiding for sleek leather. It was an instant success. That autumn, when he showed his second-ever catwalk for Bottega Veneta, wholesale orders had already tripled. "Everyone was making a frame bag," Kering CEO François Henri-Pinault told the *New York Times*. "He absolutely went against the trend. It was a brilliant idea." Rihanna, Rosie Huntington-Whiteley and Kylie Jenner were among the handbag's fans – posting photos of themselves with the clutch on social media soon after. While Maier rejected the idea of an "It" bag, Lee embraced it.

That season, it was hard to see street style photos or attend a fashion show where Lee's Bottega Veneta handbags and shoes weren't worn by the attendees. And that's because, as the second collection hit the catwalk, his first was on the racks at Bottega Veneta stores, where the pieces were selling like hotcakes. Lyst, the global fashion search engine, named the Pouch the fifth biggest womenswear product for Q2 (second quarter) of 2019. And, according to Kering's Q3 (third quarter) report from 2019, sales were up nearly 10 per cent, with most of that increase coming from the brand's stores, and the Pouch became "the fastest selling bag in Bottega Veneta

OPPOSITE Actor Tracee Ellis Ross at the Bottega Veneta SoHo store opening in 2021.

OVERLEAF A Cassette bag by Bottega Veneta.

history". Clearly, not a bad start for a designer with hardly any accessories experience.

Industry acclaim soon followed. In December 2019, Lee's Bottega Veneta won the top four statues at the Fashion Awards – Brand of the Year, Womenswear Designer of the Year, Accessories Designer of the Year and Designer of the Year – more than any other designer had before. "It makes me incredibly proud [that] so many of you live with our pieces in your daily lives and choose us to express your style," he said while accepting the award for Accessories Designer of the Year.

It was the biggest year of Lee's fruitful career. At 33 years old, he was conquering fashion, a dream that had started years before when he was a student at Central Saint Martins and an intern at Martin Margiela and Balenciaga. But that hadn't always been his ambition. Born in Bradford, England – an industrial part of the country – as the eldest son of a mechanic and a homemaker, Lee dreamed of being a dancer, a career his grandmother had practised. Then, he considered a career in law, given that he was a straightforward academic child growing up. Years later, after deciding to move to London, he landed a spot at Central Saint Martins, where he completed both bachelor's and master's degrees, focusing on knitwear. His graduate collection, in which he used techniques like devoré – a process in which sheer fabric and velvet appliqués are burned together to create a mixed material textile – earned him a job at Donna Karan, the famed American sportswear label, in New York.

Two years later, he was hired by Céline, climbing to design director of ready-to-wear. Although it had been suggested that Lee replace his former boss Phoebe Philo, he left the brand shortly after, and designer Hedi Slimane was hired to lead the brand instead. "Up until that point, I hadn't taken a break. I knew that Phoebe was leaving, so it seemed a good time to reassess," he told British *Vogue*. His break was short, though. A

OPPOSITE Designer Daniel Lee had a knack for working with green shades, which soon became a signature of his time at Bottega Veneta.

year later, Bottega Veneta hired the young designer, launching him into international acclaim. For Lee, it was a "dream opportunity". Since then, he started splitting his time between Milan and Paris to produce the Bottega Veneta collections.

By 2019, Bottega Veneta was synonymous with Lee, and vice versa. Much like Maier before him, Lee took a holistic creative approach to his tenure at the brand, from advertising to leather goods, bringing forward a youthful yet tough vision that brought the house's codes to the twenty-first century, while creating new ones. With his arrival at Bottega Veneta, he also brought a set of values he was unwilling to compromise. Sustainability, for example, is a concept he thought of through the lens of durability. "I want to make things that last forever, I'm not interested in anything less," he told British *Vogue*.

By the time Lee presented the Autumn/Winter 2020 collection – his third for the brand – fans could already spot his Bottega Veneta a mile away. It was all in the mix of neutral and bold colours, the relaxed yet elevated styles and the innovative *intrecciato* details found throughout the collection. But Bottega Veneta was still an accessories and leather goods brand and while Lee certainly brought the clothes a fresh air, it was the accessories that garnered unprecedented mass acclaim.

Take, for example, the Jodie bag, an *intrecciato*-woven handbag that features a knot on the top handle, which debuted in the Spring/Summer 2020 collection and got its name from a photo of actor Jodie Foster protecting her face from a paparazzi camera with a Bottega Veneta handbag. Although it first debuted in a maxi version, it was the mini that became a viral hit. The Jodie represents much of what Daniel Lee envisioned for Bottega Veneta: a bag that features its nods to the past, with *intrecciato* weaving, but features its youthful spirit too. As seasons progressed, the brand introduced non-leather versions of the Jodie, too, with textiles like suede and rubber, as well as

non-*intrecciato* ones in shearling metallic calfskin. It became a favourite of celebrities, influencers and fashion editors, including Kendall Jenner, Hailey Bieber and Elsa Hosk.

The Autumn/Winter 2020 collection also exhibited Lee's consistent pursuit of elegant-yet-comfortable clothing. Moving away from the brand's usual leather styles, he placed an emphasis on jersey and knitwear, including a lime green sequined draped dress, a knit maxi dress styled with a fringe skirt and oversized handbag, and a sheer black turtleneck dress styled with a crossbody bag. The high-low, day-to-night styling made Lee's statement clear: these are clothes meant for living, not for parading wealth.

"I like to design with boundaries, so the concept of the wardrobe gives a sense of parameter to the process," Lee told *Cultured* in 2020. "For me, it's about categorizing clothing and then working within each category to design garments with purpose, functionality and use."

That spring, Lee presented the brand's Resort 2021 collection. Although mid-season lineups are not meant to make bold statements, he had already shown that rules were not his thing. A splash of brown, light purple, green and red appeared as the collection was unveiled, with colourblocked styling and monochrome scarlet ensembles. Yet, it was the greens – shown in knit tops, *intrecciato*-nodding prints and handbags that hinted at Bottega Veneta's next big thing: a green mirage.

OPPOSITE An Autumn/Winter 2020 look featuring lug boots, a staple of the Daniel Lee era.

BOTTEGA GREEN

HOW A COLOUR BECAME A LOGO

Daniel Lee's Bottega Veneta was already known for its intricate use of colour by 2020. Even if the designer had been at the brand for a little over two years, his approach to colour had turned Instagram feeds and street style slideshows into a rainbow display. Yet, no other colour is more synonymous with Daniel Lee's Bottega Veneta than "Bottega green".

The shade, which is similar to what Pantone calls a "Kelly green" – was reintroduced by the designer in the house's Spring 2021 collection, transforming fashion since it appeared on the catwalk, and essentially defining Lee's era at the brand. Although "Bottega green" is not Lee's invention – early work from the brand used similar hues on leather goods and shoes sparingly – the designer used the shade to awaken the "sleeping giant", as he once referred to Bottega Veneta, transforming the brand's stealth wealth approach.

OPPOSITE Kaia Gerber walking the Bottega Veneta Autumn 2020 runway show.

ABOVE The Bottega green mini Jodie bag became one of Daniel Lee's biggest hits at Bottega Veneta.

It was October 2020, a gruesome autumn amid the coronavirus pandemic, and Bottega Veneta was staging its first salon-style catwalk, which took the brand to London. From the first look, the vision was clear: Kelly green was the new "It" colour. So much so that, soon after the show, people started calling it Bottega green. Models walked in a green-lit room, which fashion critic Vanessa Friedman described as "eerie", wearing clothes and accessories in the same shade, including tweed jackets and skirt suits, while others sported pops of green with stark white dresses. The scene was apt to the mood of the moment: Lee and his team worked on the collection in a year that had been scarred by a global health emergency but which now seemed to have a brighter future as new, life-saving vaccines rolled around.

While Lee chose green as the defining hue of his collection, it did not appear out of the blue. Colour trends for the season were drenched in green, from Pantone's Green Ash, a pastel green inspired by the increase in outdoor activities amid the pandemic, and Willow, a yellow-green shade rooted in nature. A colour often associated with evil and witchcraft, green was this time taking on its hopeful meaning, with fashion trends aligning with people's desires for an optimistic spring. Although it's also often deemed a hard-to-pull-off colour, the era of "dopamine dressing" – a term used during the pandemic to describe the chromatic explosion observed in fashion trends

LEFT A model leaving the Bottega Veneta Spring/ Summer 2022 presentation in Detroit, Michigan.

RIGHT A look from the Bottega Veneta Spring/Summer 2022 show.

OPPOSITE A model walking the Spring/Summer 2020 runway show with a Kelly green Cassette handbag.

OPPOSITE Bottega
green quickly took
over street style
photos in the
early 2020s.

OVERLEAF Models
walk the Bottega
Veneta Spring/
Summer 2022 show.

around that time – did not hold back, making way for Lee's Bottega green to dominate the year. Lee seemed to be wanting some hope too. And his instincts were correct. Bottega green was the shade of 2021, and ultimately – similarly to the *intrecciato* weave – became the brand's de facto logo.

The year was an explosion of green. Bottega Veneta bet big on the shade, featuring it in everything from Cassette and Jodie bags to puddle boots – a hit for Lee's Bottega Veneta – and utilitarian rubber slides. It added playfulness to the otherwise uppity accessories that the brand had paraded for years before Lee's tenure, as well as to the house's branding, with the hue featured on shopping bags and ad campaigns. Take, for example, the Wardrobe 01 campaign – dropped in June 2021 for a mid-season collection – featuring Venezuelan singer Arca posing before a white background and wearing a Bottega green halter dress. A clear image of Bottega Veneta's focus on green.

The shade also achieved viral popularity for the brand at a time when it was moving away from the internet itself. A few days into 2021, Bottega Veneta deleted its social media presence, including the brand's Instagram and Facebook accounts, a bold move for a luxury house that was betting big on the frenzy of its products. It was a move that aligned well with Lee's own approach to social media. "I look at Instagram and social media sometimes, but I think too much can be quite dangerous and detrimental to the creative process," he told *Cultured*. "Everyone seeing the same thing is not healthy or productive. It doesn't breed individuality."

Yet, in an ironic twist, it was hard to scroll through social media feeds without seeing Lee's Bottega green. By leaving social media, Bottega Veneta was leaving promotion up to its fans, which included celebrities, influencers and fashion insiders. Influencers wore it – sometimes sporting two matching green accessories from the brand. *W Magazine*

shot the Puerto Rican singer Bad Bunny in a green-themed editorial, which resembled the brand's Spring/Summer 2021 catwalk show, wearing a suit from Bottega Veneta. Fashion editors were photographed wearing head-to-toe Bottega green outfits during fashion weeks around the world. Insiders like MyTheresa's Tiffany Hsu posted photos on Instagram wearing a green corset belt from the brand. The rapper A$AP Rocky also took to Instagram to share a fuzzy jacket and matching sunglasses outfit in Bottega green. It was inescapable.

For the Pre-Fall 2021 collection, Bottega green continued its evolution: a halter dress covered in paillettes, feather-embellished pants, a belt-corset hybrid, a furry coat, a tracksuit and sneakers – all in Bottega green. The lineup took Bottega Veneta's codes – both old and new – into streetwear territory and mainstream popularity, showing that there's no limit to where Bottega green can go. Yet, when the brand presented its Autumn/Winter 2021 collection later that year, Bottega green was not in sight. In its place were luscious shades of red, bulbous fringed coats in beige and teal, head-to-toe feather ensembles in a grape-like purple and zebra-print accessories and clothes. A hard stop amid the saturation.

Could Bottega Veneta continue to replicate its viral success without its precious green shade?

Still, the viral phenomenon of Bottega green brought in big money to Bottega Veneta's parent company, Kering. According to the company's 2021 report, Bottega Veneta's revenue surpassed €1.5 billion, growing by 24 per cent from the previous year. Lee had done it again, and he had Bottega green to show for it.

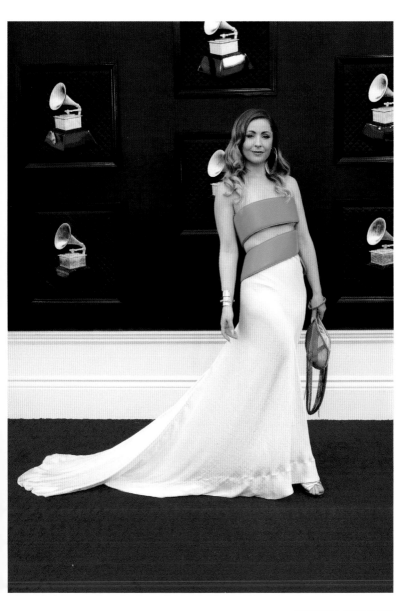

BACK TO BASICS

MATTHIEU BLAZY TAKES THE REINS

By the end of 2021, Daniel Lee had secured another successful year at Bottega Veneta. Sales were soaring, the brand was a must-have and the fashion industry had crowned Lee its new "It" boy.

He had also been nominated for two CFDA Awards in the categories of International Women's Design of the Year and International Men's Designer of the Year. After a stint of back-to-back hit collections and fast-selling accessories that were bringing Bottega Veneta its overdue acclaim, the industry expected the designer to continue delivering for years to come. He was on a roll, or so it seemed.

In November 2021, Kering shocked the industry when it announced Lee would be departing Bottega Veneta. "Bottega Veneta and Daniel Lee are announcing their joint decision to end their collaboration," read a press release from the company. No further details about Lee's departure were provided at the time.

OPPOSITE Singer and mogul Rihanna wearing Bottega Veneta at the premiere of the Savage X Fenty Vol. 3 show in 2021.

OPPOSITE Daniel Lee
and singer-songwriter
Mary J. Blige at the
Bottega Veneta
Spring/Summer 2022
show in Detroit.

OVERLEAF Mary J.
Blige at the Bottega
Veneta runway show
in Detroit, Michigan.

A few weeks before the announcement, Lee had presented Bottega Veneta's Spring/Summer 2022 collection in Detroit, another bold move for the rule-breaker, with guests including Mary J. Blige and rapper Lil' Kim. "Why Is an Italian Luxury Brand Having a Show in Michigan?" wondered fashion critic Vanessa Friedman in her review of the collection. The answer wasn't so simple. Turns out, Lee had been obsessed with the American city ever since he stumbled upon it in 2015 after travelling back from Jamaica. The show also marked the opening of a new Bottega Veneta pop-up in the city that would include pieces from the brand, as well as from local artists. The collection was also inspired by Detroit and Lee wanted to stage it at the root of his musings. In turn, he had people from all over the world, including the rapper 070 Shake and singer Kehlani, as well as the young designers Hillary Taymour and Peter Do, fly into a city that has notoriously faced some dramatic economic downturns and that would otherwise not be in fashion insiders' travel plans, especially right after Paris Fashion Week.

There, Lee played all of his greatest hits – Bottega green, lug soles, bold colours against muted canvases, fringe, knitwear basics and paillette-covered dresses – and applied them to the staples of American sportswear, from parkas and double-denim to tennis dresses and sneakers. He flexed his sportswear muscles, which he got a chance to train during his time working for Donna Karan at the beginning of his career. Some intricate techniques were at play too: scrunched sleeves were held up with metal sewn into canvas and cotton, for example. The result was the sportiest collection Lee had put on for Bottega Veneta since taking over the house, cementing once again his desire to take the once-stuffy brand into new territory, and showing he wasn't a one-trick designer.

A big splash also served as an unknowingly farewell

RIGHT Model Kendall Jenner wearing a Bottega Veneta look and Sardine bag at the 2022 US Open.

collection. On November 10, 2021, Kering announced his abrupt departure. "I am very grateful to Daniel for having brought his passion and energy to Bottega Veneta," Kering's CEO François-Henri Pinault said in the press release. "His singular vision made the house's heritage relevant for today and put it back to the center of the fashion scene." The reason for his departure was still a mystery, though. Of course, other designers have come and gone from fashion brands before and fashion at the time looked like a sartorial version of musical chairs, but few names had achieved the financial and cultural impact that Lee's Bottega Veneta did, especially in such a short amount of time. In an interview with British *Vogue*, Lee left some clues: "At best, you have a period of relevance. To try and say something big every season? You can't do that forever."

Where could Lee go? And who could take over Bottega Veneta next?

The answers materialized fairly quickly. A week later, Kering announced that Belgian designer Matthieu Blazy would take over the creative director role at Bottega Veneta. (Lee would eventually be hired by Burberry as chief creative officer.)

Much like Lee, Blazy had not held a top job at any luxury house before. But what he missed in fame, he more than made up for in credentials. A lifelong admirer of fashion and graduate of La Cambre in Brussels, where designers like Anthony Vaccarello and Marine Serre also studied, Blazy held internships at Balenciaga under Nicolas Ghesquière and started his career working for Raf Simons, who hired him after seeing his work at the International Talent Support competition in Trieste. He then moved on to roles at Maison Martin Margiela and Céline, and later, rejoined Simons and Pieter Mulier, who is now his longtime partner and creative director of Alaïa, when Simons took over Calvin Klein in 2016. By 2020, Blazy was hired at Bottega Veneta as design director for ready-to-wear, working under Lee's tenure. Promoting Blazy from within signalled that Kering didn't want to shake up Bottega Veneta's success, but rather build on it.

Blazy got right to work.

In December 2021, before even debuting his first collection, Blazy made a bold statement via the "Bottega for Bottegas" campaign, which highlighted Italian vendors in a wide set of industries. The brand overhauled its retail stores, marketing materials and ad campaigns to give space to the bottegas, including Bottega Respighi Drums, which is focused on making musical instruments, and Bottega Amatruda, a papermaker of more than 700 years. In shifting his focus away from fashion, Blazy gave an important clue about his direction for Bottega Veneta: he was interested in making clothing and accessories that interacted with the world at large and had a strong foundation in Italian heritage.

So, when Blazy's debut came in February 2022, it was unsurprising that his approach was a return to artisanal craftsmanship – always with a twist. Moving back to the Milan Fashion Week slot, the collection opened with an uncharacteristic outfit for Bottega Veneta: a white tank top and a pair of jeans. There was a caveat, though: the jeans were actually made from soft leather, printed with layers of ink to give the appearance of denim. Other easy-to-walk-in, functional yet elevated pieces followed: coats and jackets that simulated a hump on the back, monochrome leather suits, voluminous fringe skirts paired with basic knit sweaters and slip dresses with simple cardigans tied around the waist. There were some hints at Bottega Veneta's green mirage on the clothes, but not on accessories. The designer also debuted new handbags, including the Sardine, a Jodie-shaped bag in *intrecciato* weaving that substitutes the leather top handle for a gilt-shaped bar, and the Kalimero, a bucket bag with a looped strap intended to be tossed over one's shoulder. "The idea was to bring back energy, a silhouette that

OPPOSITE Actor Kodi Smit-McPhee at the 2022 Met Gala wearing Bottega Veneta.

really expressed motion, because Bottega is a bag company, so you go somewhere, you don't stay home," he explained.

From the beginning, it was clear that Matthieu Blazy's Bottega Veneta was going back to basics. Not only was it exhibiting the classic wardrobe staples – a shirt dress, white tank top or blue jeans among them – but aiming to immerse itself in the house's craftsmanship tradition. "When I took over the job, I sat with the team and asked ourselves a simple question: 'What is Bottega? What is craft, and where does it sit in tradition? How can we bring modernity?" he told *Vogue*.

Blazy's inaugural ad campaign gave some answers to the questions posed in those meetings. With the brand still off social media, Bottega Veneta opted for a book to publish the house's winter 2022 campaign, handed free of charge to customers at retail stores. The campaign was photographed by a collective of creatives, travelling from Venice to Belgium and back to the south of Italy. "Bottega Veneta was created by a collective of artisans. This is the history, and this is how we approached the campaign: together, with many different ways of seeing," Blazy said in a statement.

That spring, Blazy's Bottega Veneta made its celebrity debut as well. At the 2022 Academy Awards, actor Uma Thurman sported a white shirt and black maxi skirt look from the brand, while actor Kodi Smit-McPhee showed up in a pale blue suit. Meanwhile, actor Sarah Paulson sported one of the fringed maxi skirts from the Autumn/Winter 2022 collection to the *Vanity Fair* Oscars Party. Blazy also made his Met Gala debut that May, dressing Smit-McPhee in a white shirt, blue leather jeans and red opera gloves, referencing his debut collection for Bottega Veneta. By September 2022, Blazy's leather jeans were on the cover of *Interview* magazine, appearing to be falling from Kim Kardashian's body and leaving her notorious backside front and centre.

OPPOSITE Kate Moss walks the Bottega Veneta Spring/Summer 2023 show in a shirt and jeans made from leather.

In true Blazy form, he followed up the celebrity acclaim with a nod back to his "Bottega for Bottegas" campaign. This time, it was New York City's Strand Bookstore – Blazy's favourite – that became Bottega Veneta's focus. Through a week-long pop-up during New York Fashion Week, Strand sold *intrecciato*-woven and sleek leather handbags made by Bottega Veneta that resembled the iconic tote bags from the bookstore – only these were $1,500. But the back-to-back salutes to local businesses and cultural touchstones signalled Blazy's mission with Bottega Veneta. "I've wanted to bring Bottega to a place where it's more part of the cultural aspect of society," he told *Vogue*.

A few weeks later, Blazy pushed his objective further with the Spring/Summer 2023 collection, his second catwalk collection for Bottega Veneta. Supermodel Kate Moss walked the show in a blue-checked shirt, white tank top and jeans – a *laid-back meets luxe* look all made of leather. Similar outfits followed: a white T-shirt and jeans, paired with a beige cardigan over the shoulders; a white tank top with denim midi skirt and fur coat; a white top with maroon leather shorts and fringed coat. Blazy also evolved fringed skirts from his debut collection into equally flowy dresses and introduced smaller fringed detailing hanging from jacquard knitted dresses. Meanwhile, delicate skirts and see-through dresses were covered in 3D flowers. The aesthetic was inspired by '90s grunge, as well as a *shopper on the go* vibe.

The handbags were certainly made for the latter. For Spring 2023, Blazy debuted the Andiamo bag, a top handle roomy bag in leather *intrecciato*, which is named after the Italian word for "let's go". The bag embodies Blazy's philosophy with Bottega Veneta, which he has repeatedly described as a handbag company, and its customers: they have places to go. Blazy also debuted the Brown bag, a leather top handle meant to look like

a paper shopping bag, continuing his trompe l'oeil technique of transforming regular objects into luxurious pieces.

For the show, Blazy collaborated with Gaetano Pesce, whose 50-year career has ranged from architecture to urban planning and industrial design. Blazy and Pesce worked on custom resin flooring for the catwalk, which resulted in a whimsical show of colours, as well as 400 chairs for attendees. "The idea was to represent different characters and put them in the landscape of

LEFT Simple shopping bags were a highlight of the Spring/Summer 2023 Bottega Veneta collection.

OPPOSITE Matthieu Blazy focused on reinterpreting basics for his first few Bottega Veneta collections, as seen in this look from the Spring/Summer 2023 collection.

Gaetano," he said. Later, the custom Pesce chairs were featured in the Bottega Veneta winter 2022 campaign, featuring Kate Moss, and were sold at the global forum Design Miami.

The collection was soon featured on the cover of *Vogue* and British *Vogue*, with actors Florence Pugh and Taylor Russell gracing the magazines in Bottega Veneta ensembles. Pugh sported a blue dress with brass detailing on the shoulders, while Russell wore a red ensemble with matching gloves covered in 3D flowers.

For Spring 2023, Blazy took Bottega Veneta even further to its roots, rounding up opening his trilogy of "Italia" shows. "I loved the idea of the parade in Italy; a procession, a strange carnival, a crowd of people from anywhere and everywhere and yet somehow, they all fit and go in the same direction," he wrote in the show notes. Once again, he delivered the house codes he's worked on for the past few seasons: trompe l'oeil leather pieces, opening the show with a similar look to his inaugural collection. This time, it went beyond jeans to pinstripe shirts, feather-like detailing, flannel-looking pyjamas and sock-shoe hybrids. Having wowed in the ready-to-wear and handbags departments, Blazy focused on footwear for Fall 2023. Take the Canalazzo boot, for example, an over-the-knee number that features *intrecciato* weaving, which appeared in bold maroon and red hues.

In a few seasons, Blazy's Bottega Veneta was achieving what no other creative director at the house could before: fashion-forward ready-to-wear that is just as popular as the accessories. And it was working in terms of sales too. In 2022, Kering reported that Bottega Veneta's revenue increased to €1.7 billion, an increase of 16 per cent from 2021, while sales from the brand's retail stores rose by 15 per cent.

Blazy's artisanal-meets-commercial approach had proved a confirmed triumph.

OPPOSITE Actor Margot Robbie wears Bottega Veneta by Matthieu Blazy in 2022.

THE FUTURE OF BOTTEGA VENETA

In the coming decades, Bottega Veneta will inch closer to its 100th anniversary, but right now, it's at half-time. Since Daniel Lee and Matthieu Blazy took over the creative direction for the brand, all the elements that make up Bottega Veneta's history have finally come together: the artisanal with the commercial, the leather goods *and* ready-to-wear, the quiet and the bold. The unprecedented success from its last two creative directors also has much to do with a wider industry focus back to wearable clothing, moving away from the gimmicks and performance that had taken over fashion during the 2010s. Instead, fashion is going back to its roots, asking itself, *What makes good clothes?* Lee and Blazy answered the question with provocative work that also managed to break into pop culture – and sell like never before.

But Bottega Veneta's future will likely depend on more than a creative director's talent and creative approach. In an industry concerned with its own survival amid climate change and rising costs of living, Bottega Veneta will have to rethink how it positions itself as a brand of stealth wealth. Many of its artisanal techniques are rooted in the sustainable ethics of durability, but its use of animal leather will undoubtedly be a point of discussion in the future as other forms of leather – from cacti to apple and mushroom – continue to emerge. Then, there are its hefty prices – skirts from Blazy's debut collection were sold for over $30,000 – which make the brand an unattainable one, an ironic fact considering Blazy's wish to blend in more cultural elements from everyday people. And even the rich withhold their money during times of crisis.

Yet, Bottega Veneta's history has shown that even a brand with such a strict ethos can still have room for change. Blazy, for example, started to get playful with the brand in 2023, releasing a dinosaur-shaped figurine made from *intrecciato-*

OPPOSITE Actor Michelle Yeoh attending the Academy Awards Governors Awards presentation in 2022.

woven leather and a chip cone in the house's signature weaving that was first shown in the Pre-Fall 2023 lookbook. He also introduced the company's first-ever brand ambassador: the Korean artist RM from the K-pop band BTS. The brand also quietly started returning to social media, reactivating its account on Weibo, a Chinese social networking platform. Bottega Veneta also released a fanzine dedicated to the supermodel Kate Moss, which featured scanned images of a ring binder from Blazy's teenage years.

As new collaborators, designers and business people take over the brand, its way of showcasing Italian craftsmanship will also continue to evolve, much as is true for its past designers over the brand's nearly 60 years – from Laura Moltedo and Edward Buchanan's tenure and Giles Deacon's brief stint to Tomas Maier's stealth wealth era and Daniel Lee's mainstream boom. And, of course, all of this owes a debt to the crafty artisans who did their best with the machines they had at the time back in the 1960s, unknowingly revolutionizing fashion with their braiding technique. For all the public personas that have made Bottega Veneta the international force it is today, ultimately it's the artisans, designers and craftspeople behind the scenes who have forged its future. At a time when fashion is so concerned with its own purpose and direction, Bottega Veneta may have had the clues all along.

And it all started in that little Venetian shop.

OPPOSITE A look from Bottega Veneta Spring/Summer 2023 runway show.

INDEX

CREDITS

The publishers would like to thank the following sources for their kind permission to reproduce the pictures in this book.

Alamy: Abaca Press 13; /Zuma Press 10, 51

Getty Images: Craig Barritt 108; /Craig Barritt/Getty Images for Bottega Veneta 138-139; /Dave Benett 53; /Edward Berthelot 110-111, 122; /Victor Boyko 103; /Giuseppe Cacace/AFP 90; /Gareth Cattermole 75; /Jean Catuffe/GC Images 140; /Paolo Cocco 60, 62-63, 64; /Edward Berthelot 36; /Vittorio Zunino Celotto 32, 74, 84, 86-87; /Stefania D'Alessandro 38-39; /Pietro D'aprano 85, 116; /Estrop 144; /Fairchild Archive/Penske Media 83; /Gotham/GC Images 150; /Steve Granitz/WireImage 77; /Jeffrey Greenberg/UCG/Universal Images Group 14-15; /Frazer Harrison 80; /Frazer Harrison/Getty Images for The Recording Academy 131; /Peter Kramer 65; /Christopher Lane/Contour 92-93; /Claudio Lavenia 126; /Davide Maestri/WWD/Penske Media 71, 82; /Kevin Mazur/WireImage 35; /Kevin Mazur/

Getty Images for Rihanna's Savage X Fenty Show Vol. 3 Presented by Amazon Prime Video 124; /Emma McIntyre/WireImage 153; /Mauricio Miranda/Penske Media 44, 46, 48, 49; /Jeremy Moeller 8, 98; /Lexie Moreland/WWD/Penske Media 125, 128-129; /Jon Kopaloff 12; /Dustin Pittman/WWD/Penske Media 11, 20, 21; /Safilo/WireImage 28; /Rabbani and Solimene Photography/WireImage 66, 70; /Jacopo Raule 104; /John Shearer 143; /Jared Siskin/Getty Images for Bottega Veneta 123; /Christian Vierig 99; /Victor Virgile/Gamma-Rapho 33, 41, 52, 54, 55, 57, 100, 102, 107, 113, 115, 147, 148, 149, 155; /Tim Whitby/BFC 96; /Kevin Winter 72; /Edward Wong/South China Morning Post 68-69, 78-79; /Sean Zanni/Patrick McMullan 89, 91; /WWD/Penske Media 120, 124

Kerry Taylor Auctions: 22, 24, 25, 30, 31

Every effort has been made to acknowledge correctly and contact the source and/or copyright holder of each picture any unintentional errors or omissions will be corrected in future editions of this book.